BREAKDOWN & BEYOND

A book of hope for recovery from anxiety,
panic and nervous breakdown

By Rachel David

ISBN 978-1-5272-6627-8 (Paperback)
Nielson Publishing House Ltd

CONTENTS

Introduction

Chapter One – Panic & Anxiety

Chapter Two – Lose the fear

Chapter Three – How did this happen to me?

Chapter Four –The journey to recovery

Chapter Five – Bad thoughts and a tired mind

Chapter Six – Fight in the right way

Chapter Seven – Relapses

Chapter Eight – Insomnia

Chapter Nine – Courage

Chapter Ten – Stress

Chapter Eleven – Implementing the tools and strategies for wellness

Chapter Twelve – Be kind to yourself

Chapter Thirteen - Nourishing your body with good food

Chapter Fourteen – Hope for your future

Chapter Fifteen - Faith

ℐ

INTRODUCTION

I wanted to write a book to give you hope. Hope and proof that you can again be 100% well. When I was struggling with severe anxiety, panic attacks and finally a nervous breakdown, I struggled to find the story of someone who had made a full recovery. I needed encouragement and to know beyond any shadow of a doubt that there could be light at the end of a very dark, long tunnel; to know that I could be fully well again. I needed to know that I could once again be free of anxiety and panic, with no recurrence. I couldn't bear the thought of relapses, or the possibility that I would always feel the way I was feeling, or that I might only partially recover.

So, here is such a book, because I have been free from anxiety and panic for over 15 years now, and I mean totally free! Here is that hope from someone who understands the terrible feelings of panic that paralyse and overwhelm you. Someone who has experienced the fear that grips your body and mind; the shaking hands, the racing heart, the loud pounding heart, the dry mouth, sweaty hands, nausea, and heavy, weary legs. The fear that stops you living a full life and affects everything you do. The panic attacks which are disabling and exhausting; the fatigue; the agitation; the headaches; the tension; the dark places your mind takes you; the insomnia and long anxious nights. The belief that you will never again be well; the loss of hope and utter despair and desperation, and the sensation of being in a dark steep gorge, with no way out. Sometimes it may seem like you make progress, but you soon slip back again, and with each slipping back, or panic attack, comes more despair. This anxiety accompanies you everywhere; the tension in your body is so bad you feel you cannot move your muscles. I have been there, and now I am free. That feeling of being alive, and the joy that brings, is incredible, and I believe that you can experience this too, because if I have recovered, then there is no reason you can't too. It proves it is possible.

I have called this book "Breakdown and Beyond" for two reasons. Firstly, because there is life beyond breakdown, panic attacks and anxiety, and I mean a good life; a life where you feel alive and happy. Secondly, because there is a line in the film 'Toy Story' when Buzz Lightyear is catapulted into the air and says his famous line "To infinity and beyond"(1) The joy on his face is so great, as he flies through the air, totally free and believing in himself! That is how you feel when you realise you are free from all the symptoms that have robbed you of the joy in your life. Free!

So more than anything, this is a book of hope and encouragement, as hope during those long dark days is so hard to cling to, so difficult to believe in. I want this book to encourage you to keep on going, not to give up in believing that you can be well, because you can.

This book shares with you my journey, the stages of what happened to me, as well as the way I climbed out of that steep gorge and became well. I know from experience that you will be so desperate that you will want to immediately read the 'how to get well part', so I have started the book with some of the basics in Chapters One and Two, so you don't have to wait! However, the rest of the book is helpful too, as it talks about the various symptoms and stages, and how to get well, so it's worth reading (I obviously think so as I wrote it!). Each chapter addresses a different symptom, and I share how I overcame them, and the tools and strategies I used so you can overcome too.

I know that everyone will have a different reason or reasons for struggling with anxiety, and sometimes there doesn't even appear to be a reason that you can think of at the time. The path to finding yourself in this awful place may differ from my journey, but the destination of despair, helplessness, fear and panic is the same. This is my story of how I ended up sobbing on my lounge floor, unable to work and struggling to care for my daughter. How I ended up with months of insomnia, unable to eat and with constant panic running through my body. It is also the story of how I became free, and totally well, and have remained so for over fifteen years; free from panic, anxiety and relapses, despite some pretty tough times since. As well as reading how I recovered, I hope reading my story will encourage you that you are not alone, that I understand how you are feeling and you will recognise your own symptoms and story within the pages of this book.

One thing I would encourage you to do, is not to give up. Just keep going, even if it's only the smallest step forward, even if you fall backwards for a while. Just keep on getting up, and keep on going. There's a line in the film 'Finding Nemo' where Dory and Nemo, the two main characters, find themselves in a vast ocean, with no destination in sight. They are just so small, and have so far to go, but Dory says to Nemo "just keep swimming, just keep swimming."(2) In other words, just keep going and we will get there. That is how I felt, as though I was trying to swim in a vast ocean, lost, alone, exhausted and scared, with no end in sight. So just keep swimming, just keep swimming, and you will reach your destination.

Take courage and know that there is hope. I wish you well, I wish you freedom from the torment and anguish, and I hope that you find peace again. I hope you come to know that feeling of being alive again, and you are able to enjoy life to the full. My hope is that you find some relief and help within the pages of this book.

I want to state clearly that if you feel suicidal, you need to talk to someone. There are helplines at the end of this book, but please see your doctor or speak to someone. Also, if you have suffered abuse in childhood or other issues which you know are the underlying cause for your anxiety and/or breakdown, you again need to speak to a health professional. This book cannot help you to recover from such trauma, and I am not a trained health professional. I am merely someone who has recovered and has found the tools to be able to deal with the symptoms of anxiety and panic.

I appreciate that right now, doing anything seems almost impossible, and even reading this book may be so difficult for you. I know how hard it is to concentrate and I understand that your poor head feels like it is in a vice. Even while you are reading, those terrible feelings and thoughts will be running through your mind and body, because they are relentless. Just read the bits that you can, and hopefully you will find some comfort and help within the words.

The diagnosis of nervous breakdown is rarely used now; perhaps Generalised Anxiety Disorder is more common, but throughout this book I refer to my collective symptoms as a breakdown.

CHAPTER ONE
ANXIETY AND PANIC

Anxiety and panic can affect anyone, at any time, so do not feel guilt or shame that you are suffering in this way. Many people suffer with this at some point in their lifetime, so you are definitely not alone, although it might seem that way right now. If you are anything like I was, you might be trying to keep this to yourself, and hold everything together, whilst experiencing these awful anxiety and panic attacks. They really are so hard to bear, and I did not even know what a panic attack was when I had my first one. I literally thought I was dying. I had started to suffer with anxiety, but again didn't really recognise it as anxiety, just a strange feeling in my stomach, which I didn't talk about to anyone.

These feelings of anxiety became more frequent and they frightened me. They seemed to rise up for no reason, and not just when I was experiencing a stressful situation. I remember walking on the beach with this strange sensation building in my body, threatening to overwhelm me. By their very nature these sensations of anxiety are hard to ignore, and although not as terrifying as a full blown panic attack, suffering from anxiety is exhausting, bewildering and debilitating.

Suffering from anxiety on an ongoing basis can affect your life in so many ways. You may feel unable to go to work that day as the anxiety overwhelms you, or you might find that even sociable occasions, which are supposed to be enjoyable, are too much to bear. You might feel fatigued, and possibly think you are physically ill with some of the symptoms that anxiety manifests in your body.

Having a panic attack is scary. Many people end up in hospital thinking they are having a heart attack. You cannot believe that there is not something more ominous happening to you. That is how I felt, even when I learned it was a panic attack that I had suffered with, I couldn't believe that there wasn't more to it. Moreover you are terrified that it is going to happen again, and that fear of it happening again makes it more likely that it will. That is the nature of fear, it breeds more fear. Don't let this sentence scare you, as you are going to read on and learn how to break that cycle of fear.

So whether you are suffering from anxiety, panic attacks, or a nervous breakdown, this book will help you learn to overcome the symptoms and carry you to freedom. Just because you have anxiety doesn't mean you will have a panic attack, neither does suffering with either of these mean you will have a nervous breakdown, so don't worry about that, I know how susceptible you are to imagining the worst at the moment. Besides, you have this book to help you overcome your fear of these symptoms, no matter what they currently are. Once you no longer fear them, they go away.

CHAPTER TWO
LOSE THE FEAR

As I've mentioned in the introduction, my symptoms were severe. Initially the anxiety and panic attacks became more frequent. I began to feel exhausted and generally unwell, but without really being able to identify what was happening to me. After experiencing panic attacks for some time, and due to a prolonged period of stress, I felt too unwell to cope anymore. The anxiety and panic seemed to overwhelm me.

At my worst, I could barely lift a fork to my mouth and couldn't eat. I felt as though I couldn't move due to the tension. I was wracked with terrible thoughts that terrified me and I could barely function. I didn't want to get out of bed in the mornings as the thought of a day was too much to face, but I didn't want to lie there either, with the symptoms and thoughts raging in my body and mind. There was no relief, no escape from the torment. The insomnia went on for months and I felt so much agitation trying to wait to the morning, just to have to face the panic and anxiety all through the day too. I felt depressed, helpless and very scared.

So how did I even begin to get well?

A wonderful friend who had been through a breakdown, recognised the symptoms I was talking about and told me about a book which had helped her a lot.

The book was *Self-Help for your Nerves* by Dr Claire Weekes (1977) (1). You can order this from Amazon and I recommend that you order this right now. I started to read it, and decided to put her advice into practice. I also joined No Panic (2), a website with online resources, a telephone helpline, group therapy and one to one mentoring. I ordered some relaxation CDs from No Panic and read widely (when I could) about all the techniques for good mental health. These techniques together slowly brought me out of my breakdown, and totally freed me from anxiety and panic. It took perseverance, and it wasn't easy but the relief does come.

One of the most important techniques to getting well is that you have to lose your fear of the symptoms. Read that line again, it's essential in your recovery. What?! I can hear you thinking. That's either impossible or ridiculous! You may not even think or be aware that you are scared of your actual symptoms, but the more we are afraid of them, the worse they get.

Believe me, losing your fear of the symptoms does work. It isn't easy, but with practice and the right tools, it is possible. When you actually think about it, the only way that you know you are anxious is because your body gives you symptoms which can be attributed to anxiety.

We all know these symptoms; the fast beating heart, the sweaty palms, the churning stomach, the lump in the throat, the difficulty in breathing; perhaps an urge to go to the toilet. The legs or hands that feel shaky; perhaps you feel dizzy, plus many other weird symptoms. These symptoms tell you that you are anxious, and we don't like the feeling of these symptoms. We are desperate for them to go away, so we can feel better, but it's as though these symptoms want to taunt us, because the more we hate or fear them, and want them to go, the worse they seem to get. The harder we try to fight them, the worse they get. They are unrelenting and we hate the feeling of them. In fact we are actually frightened of them, because it's a very frightening experience having all these symptoms, especially when they develop into a full-blown panic attack.

I understand how hard losing the fear sounds, and perhaps how strange, and probably right now you are not even in a place where you are able to imagine doing that. Simply put, these symptoms are just the body's natural hormonal reaction to a situation, a thought, or several thoughts we are having. Basically it is adrenaline (a hormone produced in times of stress) which floods our bodies and causes these symptoms. The resultant sweaty palms or churning stomach is merely a natural, physiological reaction to this hormone. It's just our body doing its natural job, but how we hate these symptoms. They leave us feeling weak and exhausted, with legs that feel like lead, and they leave us very shaken up. When these symptoms are present all the time, we constantly have to live with the effects.

Looking at it another way, these symptoms are also present when we are excited about something, but perhaps not to the same degree. Our stomachs can have butterflies, and start to churn, or our heart can beat faster, but because the situation is one of anticipation and excitement, we don't mind the symptoms, yet they are the very symptoms we hate at the moment. How can it be that the very same symptoms can have two different reactions from us?

It's because we are actually afraid of our symptoms. We think something awful is going to happen, we imagine we will have a heart attack, or pass out, or be sick or embarrass ourselves. We find ourselves wanting to run, but we can't run from ourselves. Sometimes we don't even know what we are fearing, only that it is something terrible. These scenarios we imagine only make the fear worse, which makes the symptoms worse, and so the vicious circle continues.

The secret is to lose that fear. Books and songs talk about a fear that grips us, and it certainly seems that these symptoms grip us, and keep us locked in a vice that stops us from moving forward.

Losing the fear isn't easy. These symptoms are unpleasant, but it honestly is possible to lose your fear of them, and therefore the hold they have over you. I know it is possible, because that's what I did, and it worked. It took practice, it's not easy. However, as soon as you start to lose even 1% of your fear, it seems to equal that the symptoms ease by 1% too, and so it continues, in the right direction until the symptoms lessen and you begin to have long periods of time without them. In my mind, any relief, no matter how small, was a step in the right direction. You might feel that 1% is nothing, and not worth it, but you have to believe that it's the first of many steps in the right direction, and you have to start on your journey to recovery by taking that first step.

So I want you to start by taking that very important, yet shaky first step, and that is to accept this has happened to you, and to understand that these symptoms are not punishing you. They are simply physiological symptoms that respond exactly how they are meant to respond. Yes, they are a symptom of your anxious mind, but because they are so unpleasant, we also fear them, which increases the anxious state of your mind.

It is also interesting to learn that two people can face the same set of circumstances, and one suffer with terrible anxiety and the other have no symptoms. They may have different symptoms, such as tension headaches or other illnesses, but they don't suffer with a breakdown. Perhaps some people are more pre-destined to suffer with nerves. I am not an expert in this field, merely someone who has found the tools to recover. Don't compare yourself to others, feel guilty or think you are weak or a failure because you are feeling this way. These are just wasted emotions and you are certainly not a failure, you are ill and burnt out, so be kind to yourself and just focus your limited energy on getting well.

So, right now focus on each symptom and imagine losing the fear of it. Go on, right now focus on your churning stomach. What does it feel like? What words describe the feeling? Sour, butterflies, squeezed tight, like clothes in a washing machine? I found that it is good to find a slightly funny but apt description that you can give to each feeling. In her book, Essential Help For Your Nerves (2000), Dr Claire Weekes said that one of her patients described the feeling as "squeezing a lemon".(3) Every time she had an anxious thought, it was like an immediate response, as if a lemon was being squeezed in her tummy. I personally thought this was a great description and I related to this really well. Each time I had this feeling I tried to just shrug and think 'Ooh I just squeezed the lemon'. It took the awfulness out of it.

Now focus on your beating heart. Yes, it's beating fast, but try and see if you can breathe more slowly and deeply and slow it down. Think about being kind to your heart, soothing it to slow down. Don't worry about it beating fast, mine beat fast for weeks, and I'm still healthy and well. Tell yourself you are healthy and well and if you just be kind to yourself, your heart will appreciate it. Sometimes I found myself rubbing the outside of my heart area, gently, as though I was literally soothing it. Lose the fear of thinking that something terrible is going to happen to your heart. As I said I am still alive and well fifteen years later.

What about the lump in your throat? I know you think something is stuck, but it really isn't. There is nothing there. I don't really understand why it physically feels like you can't swallow, but again, this 'lump' disappears when you stop worrying about it. When you focus on it, is it really that bad, or can you learn to live with it for a while? You have to learn to live with these symptoms and ignore them. If you find it difficult to eat, just stick with soft foods for a while. I ate lots of mashed potatoes, and yoghurts!

Now turn your attention to your breathing, I know this symptom is really hard as you totally believe you can't breathe when you are having an anxiety or panic attack, and you think you will therefore pass out or die. However, your body will always fight to breathe, it's a natural process, because your body wants to stay alive, and so you won't stop breathing. When you next experience an episode of feeling like you can't breathe, relax all your body, almost slump, and concentrate on breathing in for the count of five and out for the count of five. Yes, you can do it, I know you think you can't, but count now, practise, 1, 2, 3, 4, 5 and out, 1, 2, 3, 4, 5. Keep going, over and over, slowly and deliberately. Relax as much as is possible, even if this is only for a few seconds, it will just give you that small percentage of relief, and it is these moments of relief that you need to build on more and more. You will continue to breathe, so getting your mind to believe this and losing this fear will start to bring your breathing back to normal.

What about your tense muscles? I literally felt as though I couldn't stand up straight. I remember walking around slightly bent over, as my body felt so wracked with tension I didn't think I would be able to stand up straight. I felt as though my joints were seizing up with the tension. The Tin Man in the Wizard of Oz (4) comes to mind! For this symptom, start to picture yourself as a rag doll, with floppy limbs. Visualisation is such a good tool for relieving some of the tension. Literally imagine yourself walking down the road, floppy and relaxed. You can get so much better through visualisation.

What about shakiness? I frequently felt as though the inside of my body was literally shaking, although this was not visible on the outside. Sometimes though my hands would appear shaky, and there were one or two times when my body began to shake uncontrollably, and all I could do was to try and relax as much as I could until the shaking subsided. I understand that this is frightening and again, breathing through this, imagining yourself floppy, and just accepting the shakiness and not worrying about it, is the key to stopping this.

So, firstly you need to lose the fear. This is the main key to your recovery. You might not have even considered you are frightened of each symptom. In fact you may not have been able to identify all the individual symptoms, you have just been feeling terrible.

Whilst writing this, I can't stress enough how I understand how difficult you will think this all is. Even now I can imagine you feeling overwhelmed, that this is just too much to even contemplate, that you are too weary and frightened to believe this will work, or to even have the energy to start it. Nevertheless, I also know you are desperate to get better, and however hard this is, you can summon up the smallest amount of courage to take these first steps. You can also know and believe that this works because I am proof of this.

So, go through each symptom you experience personally, as they may not be listed here. Some other symptoms are discussed later in this book. Next, whilst focussing on that symptom ask yourself, what's the worst that can happen, and is that 'worst' so terrible? Describe to yourself how it feels, and then reassure yourself in your own way. Each time these symptoms become worse, remember that reassurance, or that statement you have come up with such as "it's my washing machine churning" or it's the "lemon being squeezed". (5) Try and take the fear out of it.

I know that you want to fight, to hold it all together, to grit your teeth and fight with all you've got, trying your best to carry on through this bewildering place in which you find yourself, but this is exhausting. The way you fight this is different. It's not about clenching your fists, or gritting your teeth, it's actually about letting go. There's something so scary about letting go, as we fear that something unspeakably terrible will happen if we let go. Pretending we are ok is so

21

tiring. I couldn't even begin to describe to anyone how bad I was feeling, I just wanted to try and stay in control, but I felt so out of control.

Letting go is about going through your daily life, with the symptoms present, but in a relaxed way, almost a floppy way, accepting the symptoms are there, but giving them no attention. I used to think about my symptoms like a stroppy child; they are there vying for your attention, doing their best to make your life a misery, but you just ignore them, and when they realise that whining won't get them their own way, they begin to leave you alone. It may take some time, but they will eventually get the message!

I also know that you are probably plagued with unpleasant, scary and awful thoughts. These are usually present most of the time and make your mind fatigued. They replay over and over again in your head and this is frightening and exhausting. You cannot escape from them, you long to run away from them, but there is nowhere to run. You are tormented by these thoughts and long to be free. The same principle applies as before, you have to lose your fear of the thoughts and the symptoms they bring. Many times these thoughts are not true anyway. We believe them, and are convinced they are true, but if we were well, we would not dwell on them very much. I have written a chapter on thoughts (Chapter 5) as they are difficult to get rid of, and often linger once the other physical symptoms are reducing.

You might be suffering from other symptoms, and may come across them later in the book.

Conversely, you may not be suffering from some of these symptoms, so please don't start to worry that you will. You may never suffer from all of them. I know you will have a tendency to worry that you will, because you are scared things might get worse, but again don't waste energy on this, focus your energy on getting well instead.

So that's the basics. You can start to practise right now, and keep practising throughout the book (and beyond!). There are so many more things I did to recover, and there is much more to say on these recovery tools, so please read on and I hope you find the relief you need. Once again, these tools do work, I am proof of that. You may not believe it, but the truth is that you can find the courage within yourself to learn these tools, and you will be well if you believe in them and practise them. If I can be well, so can you!

∂

CHAPTER THREE

HOW DID THIS HAPPEN TO ME?

$\mathcal{D}$

I'm sure this is a question you have asked yourself over and over; how on earth did I end up here? It is bewildering and baffling. Obviously if you'd seen it coming, or understood the magnitude of what was going to happen, you would have made changes, tried to prevent this terrible time in your life.

I asked myself this question over and over, how did this happen to me? This question went round and round in my head, as if I was in total disbelief that this had happened to me. I came to understand that dwelling on this question does not particularly aid in the recovery process, especially if like me you can be hard on yourself at times. It does however make you aware of why you finally 'broke down' so you can address this and hopefully either seek professional help, or put strategies in place for the future.

For me, like many people, life was busy. I was a working Mum with a 3 year old, battling a dependency on painkillers, possibly an addiction, due to pain from a car accident I had been involved in, many years before. My husband and I were undertaking a massive DIY project on our house, which meant no kitchen, no bathroom and chaos in most of the rooms. During the middle of this, my Dad had a serious angina attack and ended up in hospital 30 miles away, having an angioplasty. I started having strange feelings of fear and 'butterflies' in my stomach. They would come and go, and I wasn't sure what was causing them, only that they made me feel panicky and unsure I could cope. I had no idea they were anxiety attacks. I remember once telling my husband that I felt like I couldn't cope, and he just looked around at the chaos and said "What do you expect me to do about it?" It had been difficult for me to admit that I couldn't cope, being someone who rarely asked for help, and who tried very hard to be independent and self-sufficient, and so the words stung. I determined (stupidly) that I wouldn't complain again, and told myself I could cope, and I would in effect 'put up and shut up'. Looking back this was a mistake, I needed help, I certainly needed rest, and I was only coping due to the painkillers I was taking every day.

The only way I could get through the day and cope with the pain was to take a mix of codeine, paracetamol, hyoscine and caffeine. As soon as I woke up I would take two tablets, followed by a further two later in the day if the pain didn't subside enough. I felt spaced out, but relieved not to have the pain and feeling of nausea that the pain brought. I took my daughter to the zoo, and the park, I worked; I volunteered at church, and tried to continue life normally, all whilst the anxiety attacks worsened. I felt tearful and unable to cope, but didn't know who to turn to. I had loads of friends, but over the years I seemed to have convinced them I was so capable. I stupidly didn't want to admit how I was feeling, and wasn't sure how to describe it either. I felt ashamed, guilty and overwhelmed.

One night I awoke in the middle of the night with terrible palpitations, dry mouth, pins and needles in my hands, and a tight chest that felt like I couldn't breathe. I was sweating, felt sick and seriously thought I was going to die. I curled up in bed trying to work out what was happening, and then suddenly had terrible stomach cramps and had to rush to the bathroom. I sat on the toilet in a state of shock for about 30 minutes, feeling unable to move and continuing to believe I might die. I started to panic that I might have overdosed on my tablets, not in one hit, but in a cumulative dose, which had somehow affected my organs. I knew that the side effects of codeine were palpitations, dry mouth and dizziness, and having never heard of a panic attack, I had no idea that was what it was. Gradually I felt well enough to go back to bed, but lay there in a state of exhaustion and waited for the morning.

As morning came I decided to ring 111, the NHS telephone helpline. I explained what had happened and they reassured me that I hadn't overdosed, but advised I should see a doctor. Due to the level of anxiety that was running through my body I was unable to bring myself to eat, I felt exhausted, and nauseous, and my legs literally felt like lead. Just getting to the doctors was a massive ordeal in itself, as I felt highly anxious about even leaving the house.

Sadly my experience at the doctors was not helpful. In general I think that the NHS is amazing, and I've since met so many helpful doctors, but in this instance the doctor told me I was depressed and prescribed me some anti-depressants. He didn't seem to take the time to listen, and just wrote the prescription. At this stage I didn't think I was depressed. I tried to explain my symptoms of anxiety and about my reliance on painkillers, but in my state of mind and confusion, I found it difficult to disagree with him. He insisted on giving me the tablets and said he thought I was depressed. I do think, and hope, that care for mental health sufferers has improved somewhat since then, and certainly it is better understood. However, I know from listening to my friends who struggle with mental health issues that the waiting list for counselling is many weeks. For someone with anxiety, waiting is unbearable.

Unfortunately for me, some of the side effects of the tablets were anxiety and agitation, and after taking the tablet, my anxiety rose to a whole new level. In addition to that, my body seemed to react badly to the tablets and I was sick constantly all through the night. I lay in bed shaking, terrible thoughts racing through my head, worrying that they would section me and that I would lose my daughter. I couldn't sleep, was constantly retching and in a state of panic that made my body feel as though it was locked in tension. By morning I was glad that the night was over, but too overwhelmed to face the day. My husband had to leave for work, and thankfully a neighbour took my daughter to nursery. My husband arranged for my sister-in-law to come and care for me for the day, as I was too scared to be on my own.

I rang the doctor to explain about the sickness, and he advised that the tablets wouldn't have made me sick. He also prescribed me some alternative painkillers, but when I looked at the packet, they had the same side effects as the painkillers I was taking. I decided that I couldn't face taking them, fearing more palpitations and a dry mouth as side effects. I just felt totally broken, helpless and unable to cope with anything.

The second night my husband suggested I just tried half the antidepressant, in case it had been a sickness bug and not a side effect. Sadly the same reaction happened again, and by morning I was even more exhausted, unable to face food, with anxiety racing around my body.

I would like to state that this is my personal experience with antidepressants, which is very, very uncommon. I personally know many people for whom antidepressants have literally been a lifesaver, and if your doctor has recommended and prescribed them, I urge you to follow professional medical advice. I'm sure you will find them beneficial and they will give you much needed relief. The antidepressants prescribed now are often different to fifteen years ago. I wasn't sure whether to write about my experience as in no way do I want to discourage you or make you worried about taking them. You will see why I have made this part of my story, and how being unable to take the antidepressants led me down a different path to recovery. At the time I wish I had been able to take them, and get some relief, believe me, I really wanted something!

I did return to the doctors, and was prescribed some diazepam, which probably would have been amazing to start with. However, by now I was in such a state of high anxiety that the low dosage didn't seem to help much, and I developed a fear of taking tablets in case I had a reaction again. Consequently, I was reluctant to even take them.

I therefore decided to go 'cold turkey' and stop taking my painkillers, which meant I was battling pain (and probably withdrawal symptoms too) I think I was still scared they had played a part in my panic attack, and now even taking them and feeling spaced out made me panic. I began to hate that spaced out feeling, which I had quite liked before.

So, the crash had happened. I was literally shaking; unable to sleep; wracked with panic and the physical symptoms that brings (dry mouth, palpitations, muscle tension). I had no idea what to do, where to get help, and I felt so much shame that I was unable to cope.

The journey out of this dark, difficult place seemed impossible and bewildering.

Looking back, it might seem obvious that I was heading for a crash, but hindsight is a wonderful thing! The onset of anxiety symptoms, coping with pain, dependency on painkillers and stress are not a good combination and I've since learned that you cannot cheat your body or mind. Self-awareness is a great skill to acquire. Listening to your body and heeding the warning signals, watching for your triggers and taking steps to manage these are great skills to learn and will serve you for life. However, once again hindsight is a wonderful thing. At that time I had no knowledge about these things.

Thankfully, knowledge of these things started to unfold. It was not an easy journey out of that dark place, but slowly step by step I became whole again, able to function, and with time, I felt alive again, symptom free and free to enjoy life once more.

Here, in full, is how my recovery happened, so you too can take heart, comfort and strength and begin to have hope again. I know that the briefest glimmer of hope is so important and much needed, and this isn't false hope, I am proof that you can be well again.

♫

CHAPTER FOUR
THE JOURNEY TO RECOVERY

For days I remained bewildered, wondering how I had got here, too ashamed to share with my friends how I was feeling. I knew this was probably a breakdown, but couldn't quite believe this had happened to me. I kept telling myself it must be ME, or some other illness, as I felt so fatigued. I wanted to believe that it was physical so the doctors could treat it, and people would understand. There were days when I just sobbed and felt so physically tense that I could hardly move my limbs. I was barely eating, and just waiting until I could go to bed, for sleep to take away the terror of the day. Initially I slept at night, but would wake around 2am with palpitations, the sound of my heart hammering, and a dry mouth. I would then spend hours awake, wishing for morning to come. This cycle of day and night continued for several days, while I tried to look after my daughter and counted the hours until my husband came home.

My parents were wonderful people, but they didn't understand and my Mum was ill, so couldn't really help me. When I was small they had talked in whispers about people with mental health issues and who had suffered breakdowns, and so I just felt shame. I knew that they too were bewildered by their capable daughter, now in such a state.

Thankfully I had a couple of close friends who were amazing to me during this time. One of my friends had heard I was ill and rang me. When I explained how I was feeling, she said to me, "I think you've had a breakdown. I too suffered with one a few years ago, and can understand and empathise with how you are feeling. There is a book which really helped me, and you need to order it". I still wasn't entirely convinced; I felt sure there must be some disease, or something else wrong with me, but I just wasn't sure what. In spite of these feelings, I did as my friend recommended and ordered the book.

That book, as already mentioned, is called *Self-Help For Your Nerves* by Dr Claire Weekes (1977).(1) It is a book that I read and re-read, highlighted, and turned the corners down on. It was an incredible strength to me during that time, together with another book by Dr Claire Weekes, *Essential Help For Your Nerves* (2000)(2). I chose to believe Dr Claire Weekes' words that many had recovered by trusting her methods and advice, and therefore I chose to believe I could too. That hope and belief was the first step in believing that there was light at the end of the tunnel.

I also started to be honest with myself and accept that this had happened to me. It was not Chronic Fatigue Syndrome, as I had initially suspected. It was anxiety and panic that was causing the fatigue. Acceptance of my mental health issues meant that I started to read information about my symptoms so I could understand what was happening to me.

I tried many times to really understand why I had struggled with a breakdown in the first place. Was I a nervous person? Was I too conscientious and had burnt out? Was it a product of some of the things that had happened in my past? However, it seemed beyond me to come up with an answer, and it became clear that it was better to start working on dealing with the symptoms than questioning why.

One of the first things I noticed was that many websites, books and information had a common theme, which was that exercise, good nutrition and relaxation were essential in keeping a healthy body and mind. Don't groan and give up reading at this point, I want to be honest with you and tell you my full journey to recovery, and this was only a part of the journey to wholeness. I do also genuinely understand how difficult it is to contemplate doing anything in your current mindset, with the tension, anxiety and fear filling your every waking moment. I know how taking those tentative, scary and shaky first positive steps towards recovery will need so much courage and strength. It feels like a mountain to climb, when right now even just getting out of bed takes so much effort and courage. I understand that just facing the day feels overwhelming and too much for your tired brain and body to overcome. The fear inside feels completely insurmountable, yet these first shaky steps do become a pathway to recovery.

It can feel good to start taking control in your journey to recovery, and realise that you are finally able to do something which will help you get better, taking positive steps rather than feeling helpless and stuck. My advice would be to learn as much about your condition as you can.

It perhaps sounds so obvious, but I realised that in my busy, stressed, pain filled, life, I had had no time for myself. I had not even taken time for the simple, yet essential task of looking after myself. I realised that it had been a long time since I had simply watched a film, read a novel, been for a walk, or even done any exercise for that matter. In fact I had stopped exercising several years before as it seemed to make my neck injury worse. I wonder if you too have forgotten the simple pleasures that you used to enjoy as a child or the hobbies you used to do. I was a bookworm when I was a child and used to escape into the make-believe world of a book, escaping my worries and getting carried away into another place. It was a pleasure I had forgotten. Life has so many challenges, so many incidents that cause us pain and stress that we often spend our time fire-fighting. We get caught up in the worry and stress and forget to take care of ourselves or even attempt to do anything that is remotely fun or relaxing.

So, once again I chose to believe that if all the information said that these were good things to do, I would start to implement them.

My shaky legs carried me for a 10 minute walk around the block from my house each day. I tried to notice good things as I walked outside, such as a nice garden or the birds singing. I tried to not focus on how shaky my legs were. I started taking vitamins and eating healthier food, forcing it down when I didn't feel like eating, believing it would do me good. I bought a relaxation CD (actually it was a tape in those days!) which talked me through a series of exercises which I would do every night before bed, and also I listened to relaxing music when I was feeling really tense. It sounds as though it was so easy, but believe me, it was anything but easy.

I also took regular baths with lavender oil and candles, again not easy, but I chose to believe that even a few seconds or if I was lucky, a few minutes, would mean that my brain and then consequently my body would have a break from the constant tension. The hope was that these breaks without tension would become longer.

I wasn't working at this point, in fact I was signed off sick, but if you are still managing to work, please try to implement some of these things into your evening, as I believe they will help you to relax and hopefully cope better.

Another thing I decided to implement was to write down every night, ten good things that had happened that day. It was so hard to think of anything as my mind was always inward, focusing on the tension and anxiety and so I couldn't seem to tear it away to focus on other things. However, I chose each night to 'count my blessings' so to speak. They were little things, like a smile from my daughter, or a flower that had bloomed on a plant in my house, or just the fact I had survived the day. I struggled to get to ten, but it gave me glimpses of hope, that the day wasn't perhaps all bad.

I also learned about the physical nature of anxiety and started to connect how every time I had a distressing or unhelpful thought, it would have an immediate reaction physically in my body. It was as though someone squeezed my stomach each time I had a thought that I wanted to avoid. It is like a vicious circle. You have a thought; adrenaline is released as a result of that thought; which, in turn, causes physical symptoms such as a churning stomach; dry mouth; palpitations; a high state of anxiety and tension. These very symptoms then cause your thoughts to become more anxious or despairing and the circle starts all over again. Just breaking this circle is the start to recovery.

It's important to understand that these symptoms are only natural, it's not your body letting you down, it's just the natural course that your body takes – effectively it's science. It may feel like your symptoms are unnatural, or punishing you, but it is purely the natural order of the way that our body works. These symptoms are nothing to fear. They are purely a biological reaction in our body; hormones producing unpleasant symptoms. Initially I feared my symptoms, but eventually I started to focus on each one, and told myself that it was just a natural chemical reaction. It started to take the fear out of the symptom, which, in turn, reduced my overall fear.

Finally I wrote down phrases in a notebook and read them every day. These were 'truths' which would remind me that, although my mind was telling me one thing, the truth was actually different, and that I would recover.

Some of my phrases went like this ....

Fear. What if they take my daughter away from me because I can't cope?

Truth. What if they don't? My daughter is being fed, and cared for and there is no reason they will take her away. These fears are unfounded.

Fear. What if I never get better?

Truth. What if I do get better?

Fear. What if my anxiety leads to a heart attack?

Truth. What if it doesn't? I've looked this up online and it's extremely unlikely. I am young and there is nothing to suggest this is going to happen.

Fear. What if I panic and have to run out of a room?

Truth. What if I do? What is the worst that can happen? I can say I feel faint, and will probably get some sympathy and understanding!

Fear. What is the worst that can happen?

Truth. I have no idea, but nothing worse has happened yet, and although this is terrible, it appears as if it has reached a level and just repeats itself.

Fear. What if I can't cope with tomorrow?

Truth. What if I can?

You can see that I tried to counter each negative 'what if….?' with a positive 'what if….?' I began to see it as 50/50, depending on which 'What if….?' I chose to believe.

I love this quote from Henry Ford "Whether you think you can, or you think you can't--you're right".(3) I'd rather be the person that thinks I can, and follow the route that takes me, rather than thinking that I can't.

One thing I decided not to do was to watch films that made me scared, or to watch or read the news. It is, of course, usually good to keep up-to-date with current affairs, but not when you already have adrenaline coursing through your body! Most of the news is bad news, and will either scare you or upset you. Also, it may be that you have to stop looking at links on social media, which again can be potentially misleading, upsetting or unhelpful. Googling your symptoms too much is also not a good idea! Just stick to websites that are reputable such as No Panic, MIND or the NHS. There are some helpful resources at the end of this book.

You have to start by believing that recovery is possible (and by reading this book and knowing I am fully recovered, you can believe that). It starts by taking the first shaky steps to doing things each day to break the tension. These are things that you perhaps used to enjoy, and even though it seems hard to enjoy anything right now, do them anyway, believing they will do you good.

To believe is a choice, one you have to constantly keep making.

CHAPTER FIVE

BAD THOUGHTS AND A TIRED MIND

All the symptoms of a breakdown are awful to bear, but when your mind seems to be focused inwards, and you're unable to think of anything else other than the bewildering dilemma you are in, it can be exhausting. It's as if your brain hurts. That's why distracting yourself is helpful.

As well as a tired mind, you may start to get, or already have been suffering with repetitive thoughts. These are unwelcome and frightening thoughts which cause panic and fear. These thoughts can vary, but seem so real and cause such a reaction that you listen to them. Unfortunately the more you try not to think about them, the more repetitive these thoughts become. I'm not going to disclose what my repetitive thoughts were as I don't want to plant any into your mind! You may not be suffering from these at all, so if this is the case, just move on to the next chapter. If you are, again you will know how draining these can be. It's like your mind is stuck, and is replaying these thoughts over and over. They cause so much panic. It's as if your mind is taunting you and making you think them over and over again.

The problem is that you are inclined to believe them, and think you might act on them, or feel they are so terrible that you are a truly awful person. The truth actually is that you only believe this because the thoughts cause such an awful physical reaction in your body. Next time when you think one of the thoughts, become aware of how your body reacts. Does your heart beat a little faster, or your stomach churn more? These thoughts are not necessarily a fact or the truth. You don't have to believe them or give them any authority over your mind, they are just thoughts.

The way I freed myself of my repetitive thoughts is threefold. Firstly I again wrote down the 'truths' in my notebook and read them every morning and every evening, then recited them to myself every time I had a bad thought. I basically tried to counter the thought with the truth and to contradict it. Even if you feel unconvinced, do it anyway. Stop now and write the opposite of what your thought is, or write something along the lines of 'I'm a good person and it's only my mind playing tricks on me. If I was better I wouldn't even entertain these thoughts as being the truth'. If you live on your own, write them on post-it notes and stick them around your bedroom, or on the mirror.

There are two types of thought patterns. The first consist of negative thoughts that you believe about yourself. It could be that someone has spoken words over you, or it might be circumstances that have made you feel that way. Counteracting these with 'truths' is important to stop you feeling negative and useless, so you don't remain stuck in these thoughts which make you feel like nothing is worthwhile.

Your thoughts could be "I'm a failure" or "I'm worthless" or "I'm no good at anything" I'm sure your friends would tell you many reasons why these thoughts are not true, so try and see things from their perspective. What would they say you are good at? Besides, you really must be good at something, even just one thing, so focus on that, and not anything else. We are so good at beating ourselves up, and not being kind to ourselves. Our little voice on our shoulder is great at whispering the worst thoughts into our ears and we believe it willingly! So, for example you could counteract these thoughts as follows:

Thought: "I'm a failure"

Truth: "I'm not a failure, I'm just not well at the moment and I'm going to get better"

Thought: "I'm worthless"

Truth: "I am not worthless, I'm a great mum dad, son, daughter etc.

Thought: "I'm no good at anything"

Truth: "It's not true that I'm not good at anything, I'm a great cook, gardener, accountant, brother, sister, etc.

You have to learn to be good at spotting these negative thoughts as soon as that little voice whispers them into your ear. Counteract them with your truth thought, before they spiral out of control and take you down negativity road; destination 'Sorry for yourself'.

The second type of thoughts are awful thoughts that stick and replay over and over in your mind. As I've said, these thoughts can be so horrendous you try anything not to think about them, but that just seems to make them worse. These are obsessive thoughts and are a form of OCD (Obsessive Compulsive Disorder). They can take the form of hurting others, hurting yourself, believing you are going mad or shocking thoughts about something or someone you hold dear. They are tormenting and exhausting and these are the thoughts I struggled with.

To counter these distressing thoughts, I wrote them down, and then wrote out all the 'truths' alongside them. These 'truths' were usually the opposite of what I was thinking. I read the 'truths' over and over again every day, so that they sank into my mind. It wasn't easy and it took a long time, but perseverance is key to recovery. Stick them around on post-it notes, on your mirror, in the bathroom, anywhere you can see the truth. My husband hates post-it notes, I love them! The brighter the colour the better!

Secondly, I stopped trying not to think about the thoughts, and just to let them be there. I can hear you questioning this in your mind! What? Don't try and stop the thoughts? Really? To be honest, and you'll probably agree, it was pointless anyway. The harder I tried not to think them, the worse it seemed to get. My mind was relentless. It meant accepting the thoughts; not accepting that they were true, but accepting that they were in my mind for the time being. It was about acknowledging them and telling myself that when I was better, these thoughts would not be there. It was about letting the panic wash over me, and trying to relax as that happened. To live with these thoughts and get on with my day, whatever I was doing.

I know this seems like a contradiction to the first point, but both points are about not letting the thoughts hold fear over you. Rather than trying to push them out of your mind, it's about accepting they are there for the time being, but counteracting them with the truth in a calm, relaxed way.

I can remember returning to work, still with these thoughts in my mind. The worst of the breakdown and symptoms were over, but the thoughts were the hardest things to get rid of. I was sitting at my desk with the thoughts running through my head, thinking that if my bosses knew, they would surely fire me, or certainly think I was unfit for work. However, they had no idea what was in my head, and you can take comfort from this. The thoughts are so imposing, and you live with them all the time, but no-one else has a glimpse of what is going on in your head. I once shared my thoughts with a friend, who had gone through something similar and she said to me "surely you don't believe them though, you can see that they are not true can't you?" I remember thinking, you don't understand, these thoughts frighten me, and although perhaps logically I know that, the panic means that the thoughts seem real and frightening to me.

Thirdly, I read and re-read the words in Dr Claire Weekes' books which talked about thoughts.(1) I read them over and over again, so that her advice and truths would go into my tired brain. I determined that I would counteract the thoughts with as much truth as possible, even if it seemed to make no difference and if I didn't really believe it. Again, if you can give your brain just a small break from the thoughts, your body has a chance to relax. The hope is that these breaks get longer and gradually time passes when you have no thoughts at all. What a relief that is. Now I am able to think about those thoughts and instantly dismiss them, they no longer have any power over me.

My treatment plan was a pro-active choice. A choice to write things down, to stick them around my house and to speak to myself in my head by contradicting the thoughts, not in an anxious, tense way but in a relaxing, kind to myself voice.

It was also a choice to continue to do things during the day, in a relaxing way, even though the thoughts, and other symptoms, were racing around my mind and body. To reduce the power they have over you by not giving them the time of day. Don't try and avoid them. Don't fear them. They are only thoughts, they are not the truth. They create feelings, but they are not facts.

Distraction is a great tool. Reading, watching a film, painting, crafts, baking or some other hobby that focuses your mind on something else. I know that your thoughts will be with you all the time during whatever it is that you decide, but

48

maybe just for a few seconds your mind will be distracted.

Lastly, if you are suffering with thoughts of suicide, harming yourself, or hearing audible voices when no-one is around, you need to tell someone, and get help with this. Urgently speak to your doctor, a healthcare professional or a trusted friend or family member, so that you can get some support through this.

CHAPTER SIX
FIGHT IN THE RIGHT WAY

When I began to have panic attacks, anxiety, bad thoughts, and all the other symptoms associated with a breakdown or anxiety disorder, I tried so hard to hold it all together and fight it. Surely I was strong, and could overcome this. I worked harder and harder to hold my life together, and to prove to myself, and others, that I was still capable and well. I didn't want to let anyone down, so I didn't rest and I put on a brave face. I became more and more bewildered by my symptoms, and exhausted from fighting on.

I learnt after time that I was fighting in the wrong way. I was clenching my fists, gearing up to fight my way through the day. I was trying to avoid the symptoms, and was determined to keep going; to keep fighting on. It was exhausting, scary and lonely.   No-one knew what I was going through. I couldn't admit how I felt because I was so worried about what people would think, but hiding it was so tiring and frightening. I felt like I was trapped in a parallel world, with my thoughts, panic, and symptoms, when everyone else was normally getting on with their day.

I started to learn and realise that fighting like this was not the right way to combat this problem. The way to fight was through relaxation, living my life while accepting the symptoms. I know, I can hear you thinking, how on earth can you ever accept these symptoms? They are so horrendous, so frightening, it's almost an impossible feat to even imagine getting through the day with this much tension and anxiety, let alone trying to relax and accept them. However, I can tell you with certainty that it is possible, that you can begin to lose your fear of that anxiety. Franklin D. Roosevelt said "The only thing we have to fear is fear itself".(1) If you think about it, this is so true. It is the fear, and the symptoms of fear, that you are frightened of and subsequently, it is fear that produces all the awful symptoms, which in turn cause more fear.

As I explained earlier, I did all the relaxing things I could. Lavender baths, breathing exercises, relaxation CDs, music, reading novels and exercising. However, the best thing I did was go through my day as if I was a rag doll. In fact that is how I imagined myself. Whenever I was walking in the house, or sitting on the sofa, or travelling in the car, I pictured myself as a rag doll; soft not tense; imagining my limbs as floppy. Your muscles carry so much tension during this time that it is a relief to relax your body.

So, I went through my day as a rag doll, not pushing away the thoughts or symptoms, just allowing them to be there. Allowing the fear and panic to wash over me, knowing that it would reach a point where it was almost unbearable, but then it would subside. I think you truly believe that something terrible is going to happen, but yet it never actually does. Think back to all those panic attacks, yes they are awful, terrifying, but they do subside. They build and build, and then they subside. Afterwards you feel weak, your legs feel heavy and you are exhausted and shaky. It's horrible and I truly sympathise. However, remember that this is as bad as it gets. There is nothing worse to come. Each panic attack follows a pattern, the same pattern every time. If you can lose your fear of it, and know that this is as bad as it gets, somehow they begin to lose their power over you. At the height, that pinnacle when the anxiety is overwhelming, begin to relax, let your shoulders sag, let your arms hang loose, take some deep slow breaths and kindly tell yourself that it's going to be ok, that the panic will lessen and soon be over, it can't do anything terrible to you after all.

After the panic attack I know you will feel so exhausted that you don't want to do anything, except perhaps lie on your bed and rest. This is what I would do initially, as I felt totally defeated and unable to even contemplate getting on with my day. It was as if the panic attack had taken everything out of me. However, after a while I decided to try and carry on, to try not to let the panic attack rob me of my day. This was so difficult, I felt worn out, and my legs felt as if they wouldn't walk as they were too shaky and heavy. I found however, that after a while my legs would return to normal and although my stomach was always churning, I was able to do some normal activities to distract myself.

Waking up in the morning was also a struggle. Words can't explain adequately those mornings when for a split second you feel normal and then all the symptoms crowd in and you remember the deep dark place you are in. All you want to do is pull the quilt back over your head, not to have to face the day. Tt seems like you have a mountain to climb even just contemplating getting out of bed.

Again, the fight isn't in gritting your teeth, clenching your fists and tensely getting your body out of bed, feeling defeated before you even start. You only need to begin to think ahead for the next few minutes, believing you can take one step at a time, like a relaxed rag doll. Believe that you can get to the bathroom and clean your teeth, that's all you have to do for now. Then when you have made it through, you can tell that yourself how proud you are of yourself, that you made it so far. Then believe that you can brush your hair, or wash your face, whatever the next step is. It may seem so foolish to be reading that you should be proud of yourself for undertaking such simple tasks, but you should. It takes so much courage just to get out of bed, and so much courage to take each little step. So, be proud, because each little step is a major accomplishment. Remember though, don't undertake this in a forced way with clenched fists. Instead, every step is to be taken like a rag doll, floppy but with courage.

Most days I had to get out of bed, I had no choice. My husband was working away, or out early for work and I had to get my little girl ready for school. I remember walking along the hallway to her bedroom stooped over as my stomach was churning so much that I felt sick, and my body was too tense to stand up straight. It felt like each muscle was so tense that the movements were jerky and each step was hard to take. My skull hurt with the tension and just this short walk along the hallway was immense.

Initially there were many days when eating was overwhelming too. I felt so sick, it was as though my churning stomach didn't want to accept the food. I also found it hard some days to even lift the fork to my mouth as I was wracked with so much tension. I lost a lot of weight and became very thin. When I looked in the mirror I looked drawn, pale and tired with dark circles under my eyes.

Gradually day by day I started to have less tension. It was important, and is important to you too, that you celebrate the small victories. Try to be optimistic, despite seemingly little progress at times, and especially when you have to deal with relapses. Read your 'truths' and believe that there is hope; hope that you can and will recover. Try to reduce the tension little by little, day by day, and see the symptoms start to subside and eventually disappear. Some of the symptoms do tend to linger a while, but keep relaxing, and keep believing and gradually they become less and less until they are gone.

I think we are taught to fight the wrong way, believing it is important to carry on going whatever the cost, and to be our own worst critic. We are not taught to be self-aware and recognise what is happening in our bodies, or within our minds. We are not often still. We cope with immense pressures and life altering events, without taking the time to look after ourselves. We are programmed to see not coping as a sign of weakness (well I certainly believed that) and so we don't ask for help. I have since learned that people are very willing to help if you ask.

Fighting the problem by analysing how I got to this place wasn't helpful. I would go over scenarios in my mind, and be none the wiser after hours of contemplation. Whatever the reasons, it didn't make any difference, here I was, bewildered, afraid and unable to find the way out. So, stop replaying things in your mind and focus on being well for now. When you are better you will be able to reflect more objectively.

If you suspect or know for certain that past events have played a part or caused this to happen, it may be good to seek help from a qualified professional. Otherwise, just focus on the pathway to recovery for now.

So unlearn your learnt behaviours, of gritting your teeth, clenching your fists and fighting on with exhausted determination. Just relax (easier said than done!) and take a moment at a time. Take the pressure off, and see your symptoms for what they are, a series of chemical reactions, which are a natural response to the signals your brain is sending. This response will follow its natural course and when your brain starts to relax, your body will follow, and vice versa. Relaxing your body will cause your brain to relax, and the vicious circle will start to reverse. Moment by moment the fight will become easier when you just let go.

Believe me I know the guilt in feeling that you are letting people down. I had to take time off work sick, I felt like the worst wife, and the worst mother. I believed everything would fall to pieces if I wasn't able to function. How would my job get done? What about all the administration I did at home? What about the housework? What about my daughter, she surely needed a mum who could function wholeheartedly? What about the volunteering I did at church? The list was endless. Funnily enough everything went on around me, and without me! It turns out I was dispensable after all! The house was a bit dustier than normal, and maybe my accounts got a few months behind, but none of it was really important. I even managed to function as a mum as my daughter had no clue what was happening inside of me. There were times that my mum and dad looked after her, and picked her up from school. There were times when friends came and cleaned for me. And my husband turned out to be really great.

I am blessed that I had good parents (although they didn't understand); good friends; and when my husband realised how bad I was, a very good husband. I just had to admit to them how I was feeling, and ask for their help, which was hard. The difficult times were when my husband was working away. My parents just didn't understand and I had to take my daughter to school events or her friends' parties. Coping at these times was so difficult, and leaving the house was a massive effort to overcome. At first I tried to continue coping alone, to keep up the brave fight, to fight in the only way I knew how. Learning to let go of all pressure, all expectation, to relax and stop fighting so hard was a completely new way of dealing with what I was experiencing.

Having a breakdown is humbling and certainly makes you so much more empathetic and sympathetic to others. It is a strange feeling letting go, as it goes against the grain. It is, however, only for a time. You will get back to being your old self (but with more empathy for others) and be able to resume your lifestyle, so try not to worry. Just become like that rag doll, relaxing your thoughts and body and reducing your tension. Worrying just increases the tension, and changes nothing. So fight on, but with fists relaxed, shoulders down, allowing your shaky legs to take you on.

CHAPTER SEVEN

THE RELAPSES

Many days it felt like one step forward and two back, like gaining such a small victory and then losing it again. The helplessness and despair was overwhelming. It felt as though I would never find the way out, because each time I tried, and thought I was getting better, I would slip back again. One of the worst times for me was about two months after the breakdown. I had managed to go from not being able to eat and pretty much being bed bound, to going out to friends' houses as it was Christmas time. I still felt awful inside but was trying to relax as much as I could and ignore the symptoms and carry on my days as if I was well, in that raggy doll way I have mentioned.

I remember attending my friend's wedding in December, and feeling terrible all day, just locked in tension. I wanted to run in terror out of the building, the panic was flowing through my body and my forced smiles felt more like grimaces. I got through the day by letting other people talk and pretending to be interested, while my brain was constantly reminding me of my symptoms and plight. You might wonder why I even went to the wedding, it seems such a massive thing to do when you are feeling so terrible, but this was one of my best friends and I couldn't let her down. At that point I had made some progress and was feeling a little better than during the initial weeks when I was in shock.

However, shortly after the wedding, my husband had to go away for two weeks to India for work, leaving me to care for our four year old daughter. This was extremely daunting, but I did my best to be brave, not wanting to be a burden. Yes, I was still trying not to ask for too much help – I hadn't finished learning my lessons at this point! Only a couple of nights after he left, my daughter fell out of her bed in the middle of the night. The sudden loud bang, waking me up in a start from my sleep, caused the panic sensations to come flooding back, straight through my body like an electric shock. Thankfully she wasn't hurt, but after putting her back to bed I lay awake for hours with a thumping, fast beating heart, feeling sick, sweaty and terrified. It was so disillusioning to find myself back in the same place as weeks before. I lay awake longing for morning to come. Those two weeks with my husband away were so difficult for me, and left me with another awful symptom; insomnia. As I was on my own for these two weeks, I also started to panic that Social Services would come and remove my daughter as I thought I was an unfit mother. Those thoughts tortured me as I tried to hold everything together and give her the best care I could. Of course, these thoughts weren't the truth! I was still a good mother. My daughter was fed, washed and cared for, I just felt horrible inside all the time I was caring for her, but thankfully she gave me a purpose to get up in the mornings. I remember sitting at the lunch table with her, with the terrible symptoms and thoughts running through my body and then making the excuse to go to the bathroom, as sitting at the table felt like torture. Being in the bathroom alone was also just as torturous and I realised that there was no escape, so I just returned to the table feeling defeated. Wherever you find yourself, be it at work, home alone, or with your family, I know you will agree that there is no place to go that you can run from your symptoms.

This was the first relapse. There were several relapses; I would gain ground and feel marginally better, only to find myself back in the darkest places yet again. Gradually I learned to reassure myself that I would regain ground again. Moreover, each relapse enabled me to see if ignoring my symptoms and fighting in a different way would work, which it gradually did.

Nevertheless, for many of the early months it seemed as if I was in a maze or a deep gorge from which I couldn't find my way out, and I kept finding myself back at the beginning. It was so frustrating and discouraging. I remember feeling so much despair, but let me reassure you that this is part of the recovery journey. So, each time it happens, just start again, with hope. Read your statements, reassure yourself that it's just adrenaline; accept your body is just reacting to your thoughts; do some relaxing things, and practise deep breathing and relaxation exercises.

I do understand how difficult it is to get out of this dark place, and my sympathy is with you. However, one thing I would urge you not to do, is to give in to your fears, and lie in bed locked in tension. It's so hard not to believe the fear, and to be pinned down by it. I know you will feel exhausted by the mere thought of moving from your bed, a room or your house, especially when your legs feel like lead and your body is shaky and weak. Just take one small step at a time and don't think too far ahead. If you think of everything you have to do that day, it will overwhelm you. When you are feeling this way, even managing to clean your teeth is an achievement.

People say just take a day at a time. In this case, it really is just a step at a time, and little by little you find you have done more that you could ever have imagined was possible when you were lying in your bed.

Be proud of yourself. This might be totally alien to you. Why on earth should you be proud, when you actually feel like such a failure? Perhaps you were someone who achieved a lot before the breakdown, or were outgoing and energetic. Maybe you were calm and focused. Whoever you once were, I know you will you wonder where on earth that person has gone, and have serious doubts that they will ever come back. Well, you should be proud, because coming through this difficult time takes more courage than anything else you will have had to do. You should be proud because you are trying so hard to get well, and each small step towards recovery should be celebrated by you.

Maybe no-one else understands, but I do. I know how important it is to celebrate at the end of each day and acknowledge the small steps towards recovery that you have made. To reflect and make your '10 good things about today list' (see Chapter 4). It may feel silly to do it, but please do, as it helps you realise that you are actually making progress and that not everything in your day is terrible. It is particularly hard to do when you have had a relapse and feel like a total failure. So, I celebrate with you. I celebrate your courage; your tenacity; your willingness to try. I celebrate with you those moments when you feel free from panic, even just for a moment. I am proud of you for your strength and I encourage you never to give up hope, because you can be free.

♂

CHAPTER EIGHT
INSOMNIA

Insomnia, yet another awful symptom. Not only do you feel that this is the very time that your exhausted body and mind needs its rest, but you also have to lie in bed for hours dealing with a whole host of awful symptoms. My husband would lie by the side of me, sleeping deeply while I lay there for hours, desperate for morning to come. I'm not sure why I was desperate for morning to come, because the days were horrendous too. At least there were people around during the day, even if just for some of the time.

You may not get insomnia. Each person is different, so please don't start worrying that this might happen to you. If you are not suffering from this, just skip to the next chapter.

If you are suffering with insomnia, I know the nights are a scary time. The time seems to go so slowly, and the darkness feels suffocating and overwhelming. This is the time when it is so quiet and there is nothing to distract you. It's the time that you notice your thumping heart even more. You seem to focus more keenly on every symptom until they become unbearable, as you lie awake hour after hour, alone and fearful. I lay there sweating or shaking, thoughts racing through my mind. It felt like torture that would never end. You cannot believe that your own body and mind can do this to itself. I longed for the night to end, only to have to face the day; there seemed to be no peace from this relentless struggle.

The insomnia started shortly into my breakdown. At first sleep was a relief, but this soon changed. I would go to sleep quite quickly, being so exhausted from fighting the tension all day, but then wake up at around 2 AM, after only about four hours sleep. I would then stay awake until around 6 AM or 7 AM, when I had to get up to get my daughter ready for school. It was so tempting to go back to bed once my daughter had gone to school, as the day was long and empty and I was so tired. The doctor told me to try not to sleep during the day, as it would definitely then mean that I wouldn't sleep at night. In an attempt to follow all his advice and do things right, I generally didn't go to bed. Instead I would spend 20 minutes doing relaxation exercises on my bed, but not go to sleep. Lack of sleep worried me, as I was sure that it would affect my recovery. Surely my body needed rest in order to recover. That's what I had always believed, that your body recovers during the night and that a good night's sleep is very important. I was brought up with the old saying "early to bed, early to rise, makes a man healthy, wealthy and wise". Although I still believe that, and it is proven that your body recovers and regenerates during sleep, I had to learn not to worry about it during my breakdown. It was another symptom to worry about, and one that worried me a lot initially - not only because it was a very unpleasant symptom, but because I truly believed that good night's sleep was the answer to recovery. However, as it turned out, you can recover on only four hours of sleep a night!

After an exhausting few weeks of insomnia, I noticed something. I noticed that I was able to function on just those four hours per night. Yes, I was tired, and yes I looked awful, but I was still able to function. I wasn't deteriorating further, I wasn't getting physically ill; my worries were unfounded. It seems so simple to share this conclusion here, but it wasn't easy at all. I can't adequately express how awful the night times were. You may well think that I can't possibly have felt as bad as you're feeling right now, but let me assure you that those hours lying there in the early hours of the morning were like a waking nightmare.

It may be that you are coping with work during your insomnia. Thankfully I was able to take some time off sick. However, I still had to deal with a very active 4 year old who was only at school part-time, and a husband who worked away a lot. To be honest I was too ill initially to go to work, I was in such a dreadful state. Whatever your circumstances may be, it is amazing how well you can function on so little sleep.

To encourage you further, and help you believe that can do more than you might think on less sleep than you would ideally like, I'll tell you a story about another time I had insomnia.

Five years after my breakdown, for my 40th birthday, I decided to climb Ben Nevis as a challenge. I was quite unfit, only walking short distances for relaxation purposes, but decided I wanted to do something to mark the occasion. It must have been a mid-life crisis! After a long journey to Scotland from Devon, I booked into a hostel in Fort William with a group of friends. Of course I was tired after the journey, and, as I hadn't done anything like this before, I was unsure if I was actually fit enough. Some of my friends had decided to join me, and I didn't want to let them, or myself down. I had trained, but I had no idea if this was going to be adequate or not.

After the day of travelling, my neck and back ached and I started to get a bad headache. This was not good news as the headaches were very painful and I was naturally concerned that I would still have it the next day. I also discovered that I had started my period (sorry men reading this book!). This, of course, would prove problematic on the climb as there are no facilities on the mountainside. With both these issues weighing heavily on my mind, plus the noises of shared hostel accommodation and a very uncomfortable mattress that felt like I was sleeping on a metal potato waffle, I did not sleep at all that night. Literally, not for one minute.

On the day of my challenge, I was tearful as I wondered how I would have the energy to undertake something like this. We set off on a beautiful sunny day, and it was amazing. My headache lifted, the scenery was breath-taking and I actually made it to the top! It was an amazing feeling. It made me reflect, and has done many times since, of how it is possible to achieve something, or carry on, with little or no sleep. Currently, my job means that I travel internationally, and often have to work on little sleep. I now have the confidence that it is possible to function, and even do something great, on very little sleep. Back then, on that day, I also reflected how I had actually climbed a real mountain, after feeling like I had faced a mountain every day during my breakdown. The real mountain was much easier to climb than the one I faced just getting out of bed during those difficult weeks.

I shared this story with you to encourage you not to worry. Your insomnia will pass, and you will survive this time. I also shared this story to prove that there are exciting and exhilarating times ahead of you; that life will be worth living again in the future. I am living proof of this, so please don't be disheartened when night after night you lay awake.

Learning not to worry about my insomnia, and the possible effects of it, gradually meant that again the vicious circle was broken. The less I worried about it and the less I worried about the symptoms, the more my body relaxed and sleep eventually started to return. Now I sleep really well most nights, even away from home (apart from when I'm climbing mountains apparently!)

I'm sorry to say that getting over my insomnia didn't happen overnight. I wish I could tell you differently, and I can feel your despair as you read those words. It took a few weeks for the sleep pattern to return to normal after I had decided to stop worrying about the insomnia. Just deciding to try and not worry meant that I was taking a positive step and therefore an action in working towards my recovery. Each small step is a step closer to your recovery. It is not easy, and takes practice and courage. It is so easy to get disheartened when nothing changes or you feel worse, but remember "just keep swimming!" (1)

$\mathcal{O}$

CHAPTER NINE
COURAGE

Unless you have experienced anxiety, panic attacks, depression and nervous breakdown, you have no idea what courage it takes to keep going, and to even leave your bed. As I've previously stated, when I was small, mental health issues were whispered about, as though they were shameful, and I was full of shame at the time for what had happened to me. Thankfully mental health issues are now discussed more openly, but there is certainly still a stigma or lack of understanding from people who perhaps believe "it could never happen to me". I was one of those people who believed just that, and I'm ashamed to admit that I had no understanding at all until it did happen to me!

Those people have no idea how much courage it takes to get well. With the best of intentions they say unhelpful things such as "you need to pull yourself together". Do they not think you would, if you could? They may also put pressure on you, or time scales on things, like a return date to work, or tell you what would be good for you. It may be good for you, if only it was that easy to follow their advice. Basically you may have to accept that some people mean well, but can't possibly understand. You have to take heart on your own. It can be beneficial to find a group, or perhaps online help, or a helpline, where you find people you can talk to and who genuinely understand and have the right advice for you to follow. There are some resources at the end of this book.

Sadly, most of the time it seems like you are very alone. No-one I knew, apart from the one friend who had experienced it, really seemed to understand what I was going through. If I'm honest I was too ashamed to tell people, partly because of pride and partly because of the whispers I heard during my childhood, for which I then felt shame. I also felt guilty, because I felt I wasn't able to pull my weight anymore, and just guilty for feeling this way. Shame and guilt, two awful and wasteful emotions. I know how lonely this journey is, and although I'm just the author of this book, I want you to know I understand, and I'm with you, as much as I am able to be, on your journey. Although my mum and dad tried their best, I felt very alone, as I knew they felt helpless and a little embarrassed too. That is why it is a journey that takes courage, as you share with friends and family who may or may not understand, and because no-one can possibly feel the anguish that you are suffering right now. It makes you feel vulnerable and alone, potentially judged and talked about, but take heart, because you are strong and it really doesn't matter what people think. They will soon forget once you are recovered. If people judge you too harshly they are not worth having as friends anyway!

As well as courage, one of the keys to my recovery was taking responsibility. How I hate that word sometimes! It meant I alone was responsible for my recovery, and had to do the work to take steps to getting well. On one hand it was easy to want to take the steps to getting well, as you are so desperate to do so. On the other hand putting them into practice when all you feel like doing is putting your head back under the duvet, takes a lot of courage and discipline. It means practising your breathing and relaxation exercises; it means leaving the house for a short walk; it means finding a hobby and putting it in to practice. It means finding things that relax you and actually doing them. It means practising letting your symptoms be with you and not fearing them; it means writing out your statements and encouragements and sticking them around the house, or typing them into your phone.

There are now lots of Apps that deliver motivational, encouraging or inspirational quotes daily to your phone. When I was helping a friend recover from a breakdown, I sent her daily encouraging pictures with a motivational message on. When I saw her a few weeks later she had printed them and made them into a small book that she carried around with her. I was actually quite envious and still think I might do that one day!

It also means counteracting your untruths with the truth. This is for both those repetitive, tormenting thoughts, or just the lack of hope and belief that you will ever be well again. Remember the positive 'What ifs ….' and focus on those. It means you have to practise repeating them over and over again until there is no room for doubt - even if you don't believe them initially. If you say something often and for long enough, it becomes the truth in your mind. I often thought to myself that if my thoughts could be played audibly outside of my head, people would not believe what I spent my day thinking, or the thoughts I was practising. From the outside I was just cleaning my teeth, or washing the dishes, but all the time my mind was focusing on my symptoms, my worries, my thoughts and whether I would ever get well. As the weeks went on, it became almost a game of tennis in my mind as I counteracted the unwanted thoughts with the 'truth thoughts' and smacked the thoughts backwards and forwards over an imaginary net. One negative thought would come flying across my mind and I would have to pick up my imaginary racquet and bat the thought back with a positive thought to win the point.

It also means the discipline of learning to fight in a new way. It is our natural instinct to have the flight or fight response, where our adrenaline flows ready for us to either run or stay and fight the threat. Our threat is imaginary, and there is no-where to run and no actual threat to fight. Gritting your teeth and gearing yourself to battle through the day will only make things worse, whereas relaxing through the day, whether you are working, at home, or whatever you might be doing, is the way to fight. Every small moment in time that you are relaxed, means less tension, and less tension means less symptoms, and less symptoms mean less tension, and so on. You don't have to be relaxing on a sofa or bed to be relaxed, you can be relaxed even when you are working, by being conscious of letting go of the tension in your body. You have to be diligent and disciplined at practising fighting through relaxation.

CHAPTER TEN
STRESS.

Going through a breakdown whilst experiencing stress is very difficult. Breakdowns are often caused by too much stress, and still having to face that stress can be so overwhelming. If you are being bullied or have unrealistic deadlines, or you are going through a bereavement or any other stressful situation you have my sympathy. I know that you already feel like you are hanging on by the merest thread and it's as if that thread could snap at any time. Adding to the unbearable way you are feeling it is almost too much for you to cope with.

Stress is a strange thing. Two people can be in exactly the same situation, and one feels stressed and the other doesn't. Why is that? The situation is the same, yet one person is affected and the other isn't. That means that it can't only be the situation that is stressful, but also the way that our minds perceive it. It will also depend on the circumstances those individuals find themselves in while facing the situation, such as health for example. My headaches and pain put extra pressure on me while I was going through my circumstances and it made it especially hard to cope. Rather than trying to go it alone, what I should have done was to admit this and receive help, both medically, and from friends and family. Ah hindsight!

It's so important to address the stress. This is often very difficult, because by the time you feel stressed by it, you are usually in no fit state to cope or do anything about it. We leave it too late. There is also fear of something happening if we address it, such as fear of losing our job if we complain about the workload, or report the bullying. There is also the fear of not being understood, or not being believed, of feeling ashamed. It is however, so important to seek help for the stressful situations we face. Much of our breakdown is governed by fear. Fear of never getting better; fear of the symptoms; fear of what might happen next; fear of our circumstances; fear of what might happen if we try and change our circumstances. Fear, fear, fear!

If you think your breakdown is caused by stress, or is being made worse by stress, try hard to identify what that stress is. As difficult as it is, speak to someone about it. I know this is really hard as you are so tired and weary, and your mind is so exhausted, but changing the situation will also bring relief. Even sharing with someone can be difficult, as you make yourself vulnerable. So do make sure you choose the right person. Choose wisely, and hopefully they will be able to help you.

If you still have to face the stress for now, and are not able to change your circumstances, just keep practising the strategies shown in this book, and your perception of these stressful circumstances will hopefully change as you become better. Once you are better you will be able to deal with these circumstances and make the necessary changes.

For the last five years my circumstances have been tough. My daughter has faced some significant health struggles and I have been her main carer. We have been victims of fraud to the tune of £30,000; I've lost both my mum and my dad to cancer and we have also moved house three times during this time! The reason I say this is to encourage you, because at no time have any of my symptoms returned. Moreover, although I have naturally struggled during these difficult times (who wouldn't!) I have never broken down again or had a panic attack, thank God. This is all while holding down a busy role as Director of a small charity, and travelling throughout the UK and internationally.

I've shared these personal struggles with you to encourage you that I am not just well because my life has been great, but that I have remained well even through difficult and busy times. I wrote this book to bring you hope! Be encouraged and inspired that your recovery is possible.

CHAPTER ELEVEN

IMPLEMENTING THE TOOLS
AND STRATEGIES FOR
WELLNESS

If you read the chapter on stress, you will have seen that during the last five years my circumstances have been tough. You might, therefore, be tempted to think that I must be stronger than you to be able to go through all this without breaking down again. The answer to that is a resounding no! It only means that have come through my breakdown, learned a lot and now have confidence in the strategies I learned. I still implement a healthy lifestyle, and when things get tough I cut myself some slack, rather than fighting hard.

You might also think that I cannot possibly have been as bad as you are now, and, of course, it is difficult to ever know what someone else experiences as you can't live inside another person's mind. However, let me reassure you that my symptoms, as previously described, caused me so much anguish, terror and fear that I could not eat, sleep or cope. The panic attacks were relentless; the churning stomach, palpitations, shaky legs and hands; exhaustion and torturous thoughts were almost too much to bear. I felt defeated, bewildered and full of despair. I cannot really find the words to adequately describe how awful those months were.

You might also believe that I am only well because I constantly manage my lifestyle. I guess in part that might be true, but I can honestly say I never think about it. I suppose I learnt a big lesson during my breakdown, or more accurately a series of lessons, and I spent so much time learning the strategies and tools that now I just naturally implement them into my lifestyle. They are coping strategies that have become habits which I no longer think about.

Caring for my daughter during her health struggles meant many sleepless nights, but I no longer worry about sleep. I moan about the bags under my eyes sometimes, but know that I can cope! If I feel stressed by something I go for a run, or walk, or take a few moments to read a novel, even if it's just for a few minutes. I frequently listen to audio books when I am driving and escape into another world. I eat healthily and try and look after myself. I try and look at the positives at the end of a difficult day, and often repeat quotes to myself when things are tough. I also have a faith, so I spend time in prayer. These things mostly come naturally now, and are good habits for a healthy future. Sometimes being positive at the end of a tough day is hard and doesn't come naturally, but the habit of trying to find something to be thankful for is worth it. I still get nervous sometimes, as we all do, but in a normal way, such as before an exam, or a public speaking engagement. My stomach churned upon learning the news my Dad had cancer, but again, that is in the realms of what most people would suffer and it soon subsided. It reminded me of when my stomach used to churn day after day, but I knew it would go away if I gave it no attention.

That is the secret to not having another breakdown. You will gain so much confidence in knowing these tools work that you won't fear another breakdown as there is nothing to fear – you know the tools for recovery. That knowledge empowers you and releases the fear.

CHAPTER TWELVE
BEING KIND TO YOURSELF

✍

I often listen when people are talking and I am surprised at how unkind we are to ourselves. We take on too much, overlooking caring for ourselves at the expense of others; we put ourselves down, and we think bad and negative thoughts that drag us down. We are often our harshest critic and are much kinder to other people than we are to ourselves.

Retrospection is important at some time. Once you are starting to feel better, it is good to reflect back and think about what contributed to your breakdown. Often sufferers from breakdown are conscientious, hard-working people who try their best to achieve a high standard in everything they do. They try hard to hold everything together and this can put them under enormous strain and pressure, when, in fact, they need support and help. I was not good at asking for help, even when I was ill. I didn't rest properly and I wasn't listening to my body when it was giving me all kinds of signals that things were not right. I either didn't recognise the symptoms, or ignored them. Either way I was definitely putting my body and mind under strain.

Taking rest is so important. I know that sounds cliché but I've learned it is so important for our wellbeing. We can rest mentally by enjoying hobbies and these might benefit us physically too.

87

We work ourselves so hard, meeting deadlines, caring for our families or others, undertaking projects at home or at work, volunteering, or whatever we are racing around doing. We care for everyone apart from ourselves. I have genuinely learned the hard way that unless you take care of yourself, you will not be able take care of anyone else. If taking care of yourself is the least of your priorities then you will need to re-think. We are often so unkind in the way we think about ourselves and talk about and to ourselves. We take on too much and often put everyone else's needs above our own. No wonder we struggle!

Building time and space for yourself is essential. Losing the fear of the symptoms will stop you experiencing them, but why continue to put your body and mind under strain. Your body will only start to exhibit symptoms of stress in other ways, such as frequent colds and illnesses, and perhaps over time, more serious illnesses such as high blood pressure. If you continue to ignore your own needs, emotionally you will feel exhausted. So, if you want to live a healthy life, you need to look after yourself and be kind to yourself.

Talking to yourself kindly is a great way of helping your emotional health. If you listen to the way you think about and talk to yourself it is often very unkind. We hopefully wouldn't talk to others this way, and would probably firmly tell them that their thoughts about themselves are wrong. Again we hold ourselves to very high standards. I was always beating myself up about something, which would make me try harder and harder. We tell ourselves we are worthless, or people would be better off without us, or we've failed, or have regrets. These thoughts spiral into a barrage of self-abuse, where we catastrophize outcomes, and leave ourselves feeling awful and exhausted. Again, very much like the repetitive thoughts recovery, we need to counteract them every time with 'truth thoughts' even if we don't actually fully believe them to start with.

I was very blessed to have wonderful parents who always encouraged me, and spoke words of affirmation to me. However, life wasn't always easy, I was bullied at school and my Mum became ill with a brain tumour when I was 13. Thankfully though, those early years of parenting gave me confidence and self-belief. Unfortunately I didn't inherit my parents' laid back attitude! They never seemed to worry about anything, but I seemed to worry about things happening. When I was young, I was nervous being in the house on my own, and was homesick when I was away from home. My bedroom was at the other end of the bungalow, away from my parents and brother, and I often felt quite scared in the middle of the night. After my breakdown I had to learn the art of not worrying by counteracting worrying thoughts with 'truth thoughts'. If I worried someone would break in, I started to think about how infrequently that happened. If I worried about the plane I was in crashing, I immediately reminded myself that flying is the safest form of travel. It's quite a good idea to avoid the news until you are fully recovered. It's just so full of awful articles that you begin to believe that everything and everywhere is awful, and you can begin to catastrophize. In fact, I advise that you avoid everything that is scary and/or adrenaline filled (thriller films for example!). Avoid anything that will raise your adrenaline levels, or worry levels in any way. Why fill your mind with awful news, when you can fill your mind with uplifting thoughts and words? When I was ill my husband suggested we watch Pirates of the Caribbean, (1) and I spent most of the time with my eyes closed, it was just too scary for me! I know, it's only a Disney film!

If you had parents who constantly put you down, told you that you were worthless and a failure, you unfortunately would have begun to believe what was spoken over you, and those thoughts will have become ingrained. It will be hard to break this habit now, but believe me, it was your parents who should not have spoken these harsh words to you. Every child deserves to be praised, encouraged and affirmed for something. If you were bullied at school like me, it's hard to forget the cruel word of your peers, they play over in your mind. They make you work hard to 'prove them wrong' or may have affected your confidence.

Perhaps your partner has been emotionally abusive, and you now believe the things they've said, or how they made you feel. I have friends who have experienced this. Whatever the reason for your thought patterns, and they could have been formed due to countless circumstances, we have to become good at listening to how we talk to ourselves, and start to change the patterns if we want to be fully emotionally well.

It's a constant journey to form new thoughts, and using 'truth thoughts' has to become a habit. We have to catch ourselves worrying, catastrophizing, having bad thoughts about ourselves and immediately counteract them.

The second thing we need to get good at is recognising when we start to overdo it, take on too much, or feel overwhelmed by our circumstances. The minute you start to think you can't cope, or you feel overtired, can't face your workload, or the demands upon your life or time are too much, heed the warning! Things can wait. As I've said, nothing fell apart when I was ill, I wasn't indispensable and life carried on around me as normal.

Allow yourself to take a bath, or watch a film instead of finishing the housework, homework, DIY or whatever else you feel you have to do after a day at work. Your body and mind will thank you for the break and you will be refreshed to start the next day. I know this is hard, especially if you are a perfectionist or a conscientious person. We often feel guilty about taking a break; again we beat ourselves up. This was one of my downfalls, I felt lazy and guilty if I took a break. I had been raised to work hard, and also to help others, so this is how I spent my time. Of course these are good values, but if we feel overwhelmed and stressed it's time to re-evaluate our lives. Obviously we can't spend our life just watching TV or languishing in the bath, as nothing would get done, but it is about being kind to ourselves and not overdoing it. Some people refer to this as the work/life balance.

It's very important to be honest with yourself. Again I wasn't honest with myself at all. I thought I was indestructible, I wasn't self-aware at all. I put myself on a self-made pedestal and didn't want to let anyone down. I pushed myself to the limit and I put myself under incredible pressure. I tried to do my best at everything, and I'm ashamed to say that I thrived on the fact that people seemed to think I was superwoman, and it felt good when they said "I don't know how you do it". Well, pride comes before a fall! Now if people say that to me, I stop and think, "Am I overdoing anything in my life?" I take it as a warning, not a compliment!

Life is indeed a balance, and it is a great skill to become self-aware. It means you can heed the warning signs, be kinder to yourself and be aware of how you talk to yourself. The other skill is to actually take action, as it is very easy to be aware of the warning signs yet ignore them. Ignore them at your peril! These warning signs are part of your recovery and form the precaution of never having another breakdown. Learning self-awareness, 'truth thoughts' and taking time for yourself is a gift to yourself, and others.

So, be kind, think kind, treat yourself well, because others may not treat you kindly, and may not even appreciate why you are taking this time for yourself.

You may need to become assertive, and it will certainly mean that you have to make some changes, but let me to encourage you that they are necessary and important to your emotional and mental health. So, be honest with yourself, and others, ask for help, seek professional help if necessary, and practise self-awareness.

CHAPTER THIRTEEN

NOURISHING YOUR BODY
THROUGH GOOD FOOD

Several years before my breakdown I suffered with Irritable Bowel Syndrome, (IBS) probably brought on by stress – yes I should have listened to my body several years before! By co-incidence, during this time, my husband went on a diet and we started to change the way we ate and cooked by introducing more vegetables, low fat foods and less processed foods. This had a dramatic impact on the symptoms of my IBS, which began to lessen, and eventually cleared up altogether.

My interest in the use of food as a medicine increased, and I used to read avidly about nutrition. When I had my breakdown I realised that I needed to support my body during this time of great stress. I felt I should be kind to myself, as I knew my body and mind were exhausted and would benefit greatly by being well nourished. The stress hormones (adrenaline and cortisol) can make our digestive systems struggle and we don't adequately absorb nutrients from our food, which depletes our levels of essential vitamins and minerals. Our immune systems can also be compromised, leading to frequent colds and illnesses. As you already feel so ill, fatigued and exhausted, you really won't want to be struggling with illness as well. If, in addition to your breakdown, you already struggle with illnesses, or if your breakdown has been exacerbated because of illness, then your body (and mind) can definitely benefit from some good nutrition.

After recovering from my breakdown, I decided to pursue my interest and study nutrition, and I am now a qualified Nutritional Therapist, with a Diploma in Nutrition. Consequently, I have seen the healing effect that foods can have on the body. I am a great believer in being kind to yourself in every way you can, giving your body the best chance of good health.

There are two main things that I did, which I believe would benefit you too. Please know that at first there was no way I could focus or concentrate on this, I was too ill. As time went by, and my anxiety lessened, I was able to focus on other things.

The first tip is to keep your blood sugar stable. Very simply this means that if we eat foods which are high in sugar, the sugar level in our blood is raised, giving us a short burst of energy. While this feels good in the short-term, it very quickly drops, leaving us feeling tired and even irritable. If we keep eating these types of foods, our blood sugar levels can rapidly go up and down, which is exhausting for the body. As you already feel so completely exhausted and fatigued, you don't want to be doing anything that makes this worse. Unfortunately, just when you feel like eating comfort foods, such as cakes and chocolate, this is the time you need to reduce or avoid them.

Eating too much sugar has a detrimental effect on your immune system, your blood sugar levels and your energy. That said, some chocolate or cake as an occasional treat to make you feel better, while you are feeling so desperately awful, is allowed! Just make sure that these foods are not a regular part of your diet.

Other foods that cause your blood sugars to rise quickly are foods that have been stripped of their fibre and bran, such as white flour in white bread, white pasta and white rice. They might not taste sugary, but they do cause the sugar levels in your blood to rise quickly, having the same unwanted effects.

It is important therefore to eat foods which release sugar slowly. These are wholegrain foods, such as brown flour products e.g. whole wheat or whole grain bread, brown rice, and oats.

You might not feel like eating at all, but this can leave you feeling shaky and tired. These are not symptoms you want to be feeling when you already feel shaky and tired because of your anxiety.

Proteins such as good quality animal products (not processed meats) and beans, lentils and pulses are great choices, as protein keeps you full for longer.

The second tip is to eat lots of vegetables and fruit. Fruit and vegetables are your best friends for so many reasons! I'm not going to go into too many details as this isn't a nutrition book, but

97

they are high in fibre, rich in vitamins, minerals and anti-oxidants, and are scientifically proven to boost your mood! Your body loves them! So, five portions of vegetables and two portions of fruit per day would support your body. I have listed some good nutrition books at the end of this book so you can read them if you want more information.

Here is a typical list of what I would eat on my journey to recovery:

Breakfast was porridge with organic milk or organic oat milk, plus frozen blueberries or cherries cooked with it. In the summer I now eat strawberries, blueberries and raspberries with natural yogurt. I sometimes add a little honey. I would then snack on an apple or banana, with some nuts or seeds.

Lunch was a jacket potato with a big salad, plus tuna or beans, or chicken salad, or homemade soups, packed with vegetables and lentils. I love snacking on hummus and chopped carrots or celery.

Dinner was salmon with new potatoes and two to three portions of vegetables, or a home-made curry, or a homemade stew.

Basically I made most things from scratch, making the most of seasonal, good quality ingredients, with lots of fresh fruit and vegetables. If you don't have a lot of money, using beans and lentils is cheap compared to meat, as are jacket potatoes and homemade soup.

I think it helps to feel you are doing something towards your recovery that you can control. It feels like everything else is so out of control during this time, and knowing there is another way you can support your body and help it towards healing, is a positive step to take.

In the early days there was no way I could focus on this, it was hard just to make it through the day, I could barely leave my bed, and had no appetite at all. I remember my husband being really worried as I couldn't even eat mashed potato because I felt as though my arms were like lead and I couldn't even lift the fork to my mouth. I felt as though I couldn't swallow and felt nauseous and sick. My husband was so worried about me and he tried really hard to encourage me to try to eat. I tried eating liquid type foods such as yoghurt, but it took me ages to even get half-way through one. As I've previously said, I lost a lot of weight in the early days. However, as a few weeks went by, I was able to function a little better and that's when I focused on eating well, doing some exercise and relaxation.

Eating with a churning stomach is not easy. Preparing food with all the symptoms raging in your body is also not easy, and I remember countless times standing at the kitchen worktops with panic raging through my body, and my hands shaking. However I kept practising the method in chapter one, where you carry on in a relaxed way, going through the day, learning not to be afraid of your symptoms. So, I stood, with my shaky body, my inward focused thoughts, my churning stomach and my racing heart, chopping vegetables!

If you can at least try and eat some healthy foods, every small change will make a difference. It is also a good habit to get into for the future, for when you are better. Healthy habits are the way forward for you, and it pays to be kind to your body, and to look after yourself well. I know it sounds clichéd but good food, adequate rest, exercise, relaxation and fun really do have great benefits for the body and mind.

Again, one thing is for sure, I am fully recovered and you can be too. Good food, exercise, rest and relaxation definitely played a part in my recovery. However, as I have consistently mentioned, the main reason for my recovery was to stop worrying about and fearing my symptoms. By just letting the various symptoms be present and by accepting them, it took away their power and caused them to disappear over time, until they were completely gone. The habit of eating healthily/other habits, are just great habits to help support you, and prevent stress again in your future.

If you have any existing health conditions, please seek the advice of your doctor, or other qualified healthcare provider, before changing your diet.

CHAPTER FOURTEEN

HOPE FOR YOUR FUTURE

Throughout this book I have endeavoured to reassure you that you can be fully well again. You can know a future free from panic, anxiety and depression. You have to believe it, practise it and never, ever give up hope. You may relapse, even frequently, but just keep picking yourself up, and continue to practise this advice and just keep on going. You will come out of this dark, desperate tunnel. This advice really works and I am proof that it does, so take heart and feel that hope continuously within you.

I have been honest with you and not embellished or exaggerated anything. I hope you become well, and stay well. I believe everything happens for a reason, and it will certainly make you a more empathetic person, which can only be a good thing! It means you will understand the struggles of others who are anxious or depressed and you will be able to support and help them when they are going through their dark days.

Whatever happens, do not give up; just keep on taking another shaky step. One day you will suddenly feel alive again, and it is such a wonderful feeling. I cannot fully express the joy that you feel when those dark clouds are finally lifted and your mind is clear. You do literally feel like you are walking on air! That experience is waiting for you. Try and imagine it now, that feeling of being symptom free.

One final thing which I have already touched on briefly is the power of visualisation. Visualisation is imagining yourself how you want to be, not how you actually are feeling at the moment. It is a powerful tool to help you see yourself as healthy and well once again. At first this wasn't something I was able to do, but as I started to recover it was something positive to focus my mind on. You could imagine yourself returning to work, or doing well at a presentation, or feeling great when you go out with your friends once again; whatever the things are that you long to do.

You will smile when I tell you the story of my visualisation. My breakdown happened in November, and on 1st April I was due to start a new job. Thankfully my interview had been several weeks before my breakdown. Obviously at first I was petrified that I wouldn't be well enough to start a new job, but I practised taking one day at a time. As the time drew near, I ordered myself some new clothes, and rehearsed over and over again in my mind how I would look as I entered the room for my new role. I was going to be wearing some elegant heels, and I visualised myself feeling well, and looking good! The reality was somewhat different, because on entering the room, I fell down a grate and the heel of my shoe got stuck. I then had to bend down, take my shoe off and pull it out in front of everyone; not a 'grate' way to make a first impression! Excuse the pun!

Seriously though, it is a very positive action to practise thinking about being well, and what you will do, and how good you will feel. This focuses your mind on something positive and, even if it's for a few seconds, stops your mind focusing inwards.

Please don't despair when you read that I started work again after 5 months. It could be that you have been struggling for many more months than this, or that your symptoms come and go. I found the way out, and now you can too. If you are also thinking I can't possibly bear feeling like this for a moment longer, remember that this is a journey, and the really severe symptoms start to ease once you put these tools into practice.

The benefit is that you can practise visualisation from your own home, as it is a safe space, and you can find a relaxing time to do this. I used to do this when I went to bed at night. When you have a young child it is hard to find a peaceful moment! As I have said, doing this was impossible for me in those first long torturous weeks of the breakdown, but as you recover, this becomes easier.

So, to sum up: Learn to be kind to yourself; lose your fear of the symptoms (that's the key); practise breathing, relaxation and healthy eating; write down your 'truth thoughts' and counteract those negative repetitive thoughts; visualise yourself well, and take hope. Getting well means taking action, in all the ways we have talked about in this book.

So I would like to wish you all the best in your journey to recovery. I hope you find strength and joy in your future and freedom from panic and anxiety, so you can lead the life you want to lead. From the bottom of my heart I wish you peace.

𝒮

CHAPTER FIFTEEN
MY FAITH

It wouldn't be fair to leave out one of the most important aspects of my recovery; my faith. It was an integral part of my journey back to health, but please feel free to close and end the book here if you do not share, or have any interest in my faith. I wish you well and hope that you recover soon, and have a wonderful, joyful life, free from panic, anxiety and nervous symptoms.

I am a Christian, and my faith is the most important part of my life. I want to give God all the thanks for my recovery, and I believe that God was my ever present help in my time of trouble. When I talk in the book of everything I have been though, and everything I have overcome, it is only because of God's grace, mercy and love for me that I am able to stand now. When I   re-read the paragraph about my circumstances over the last five years, and how I have never broken down again, I felt so full of gratitude, my heart was overwhelmed with His goodness. I want to thank God for His faithfulness to me both during my breakdown and during the difficult times since.

I believe that God gave me friends in my life to pray for me during the darkest of days, and the friend who told me about Dr Claire Weekes' books. I also believe that healing takes place in many different ways, and for me, this was through knowledge and putting that knowledge into practice. I had to take responsibility for my recovery, whilst asking for God to help me through.

My breakdown was, however, initially difficult for me to comprehend. I felt so much guilt, feeling that as a Christian, it shouldn't have happened to me. I believed that I should be holding it all together, and that I had let God and others down. I felt ashamed too, that it had happened to me and I didn't want anyone to know.

I believed that as a Christian I should have been stronger, or should have had more faith, or needed to pray more. One of the worst things was that at first I couldn't even find the strength to pray, and reading the Bible seemed impossible. I felt so guilty about this too, but I was in such a tense, exhausted state, just praying or reading the Bible was definitely too much for me. In the end I just had to accept that if God loved me, and created me, then he also understood. He knew that I still loved Him, but that right at that moment I was too ill and exhausted to pray. After a few days I just managed to utter "Dear God, please give me strength and courage to face the day". That was my prayer day after day after day. There were no fancy, long articulate prayers, just a few desperate words. I certainly needed courage to face the day when it seemed so overwhelming and impossible and I believe that God heard my desperate cry and saw my tears.

I found I couldn't read Christian books either, they somehow seemed too intense, and my brain felt so tired. I initially read too much into everything that was written, searching for the way out, as if the answers somehow were there, but eluded me. In the end I decided to just read relaxing novels, to switch off my brain.

I felt guilty that I couldn't read the Bible, when usually during my difficult times it had been a source of comfort, strength and direction to me. Surely I needed to read it more than ever now, during one of the most difficult times of my life. I felt it was what I should be doing as a Christian.

During this time, a lovely friend who was praying for me told me that she had been reading the Bible and felt God giving her a verse in Hebrews 12 for me "Strengthen your tired legs"(1) She told me she would pray that verse for me until I was well. How lovely to have a friend who supported me in this way, and prayed on my behalf.

I also felt guilty about some of my repetitive thoughts as they were so awful and wouldn't go away. Again I am not going to reveal them here as I know you could be susceptible to thinking them too, but believe me, they made me feel sick and shameful. As a Christian surely these thoughts were not honourable to God. However, I began to realise, in fact, that I was ill. Mental illness is just another type of illness. It's in our head, rather than our body – even though it can have a huge impact on our body. We wouldn't feel guilty about a physical illness, so why should we feel guilty about an illness in our mind? I learned to not allow the thoughts to scare me, or to give them the time of day, and to just let them sit there, although this was hard. I constantly practised the 'truth thoughts' and counteracted the negative/awful thoughts with these truths, and eventually, and I mean eventually, they went away.

I also wondered why God didn't heal me. I kept hoping that I would wake up and find I was one hundred percent well, and that a miracle had occurred. I'm sure that there may be someone, somewhere who has been miraculously, instantly healed, but I didn't know (and still don't know) of anyone. I never lost my faith and I just tried to hold on to the hope that I would recover one day. Some days it was just the merest glimmer of hope, and was so difficult to hold on to.

I think it's important to say that well-meaning Christians who have never experienced the sudden shock after the onset of a nervous breakdown can't fully understand. I would have been one such Christian before this happened to me. They might tell you how important it is to stand firm, keep praying and to read your Bible. Of course, they are right, and I'm sure you know this, but at this time it may not be possible to do this. If you are able, I would encourage you to absolutely continue, as there are so many times that God has comforted me, spoken to me and strengthened me through His words in the Bible. You can also fight your battles through praise and worship, and putting on worship music is a wonderful way of relaxing and letting God's truths enter your mind. It is another way to fight the right way.

I'm just being completely and totally honest with you, because I think it's so important to be real. I'm letting you know that you shouldn't feel guilty if you are too exhausted, bewildered and tense to do those things at first. I just listened graciously to that advice while thinking to myself, "You have absolutely no idea what I am going through!" Of course I felt a lot of guilt already about this, without being reminded of it. I also thought, at times, that perhaps if I could pray, quote verses and read my Bible that I would be well, and it was because I wasn't doing those things that I wasn't getting better. It was just another defeatist thought that brought a feeling of hopelessness and guilt. I realise now that God doesn't want me to feel unworthy, guilty or ashamed. Having a breakdown doesn't mean you are a failure. If your faith is important to you, then you will pray, read your Bible and worship again as soon as you are able to, because of your love for God and your relationship with Him.

I learned to let go of the guilt and the 'should be doing' thoughts, and accept that I am loved and cherished by God, and saved by grace through Jesus Christ. That grace is sufficient for all circumstances, and when I was better I was so full of gratitude to God for bringing me through such a difficult time. I felt intense joy and such a freedom and I hope that you experience such positive emotions after such a difficult time. I want to encourage you once more that you can be well, and once you have come through those dark, desperate days, the joy is incredible. So please don't feel guilty as well as all the other terrible emotions you are feeling. That guilt is misplaced, you are loved. God does understand and walks with us in our darkest times. When I talk about counteracting my thoughts with positive thoughts, I am referring to what the Bible means when it talks about taking every thought captive. I am talking about choosing to believe what the Bible says about me, not what I think about myself. The Bible tells me that Jesus loves me, and died for me, so that I can have abundant life. It is an active choice to keep on taking thoughts captive, and it takes practice! God doesn't do it for us. That is why I wrote down my 'truth thoughts' and reflected on them over and over again.

I believe that healing comes in many forms, and although mine wasn't miraculously instantaneous, it was nonetheless healing. Healing can come through managing symptoms, through knowledge and applying that knowledge, as well as holding on to belief that you will get well. I heard a message at church recently entitled 'Your breakthrough might be your walk through' In other words, some things we have to journey and walk through instead of having (and wishing for!) an instantaneous breakthrough.

I believe that God has a good plan and purpose for me, and loves me. You may ask, why did God allow me to go through this? Of course I don't exactly know the answer to this, but I choose to believe the verse in Romans 12 in the Bible that says "All things work together for good for those who love God"(2) I believe that we go through everything for a reason, and upon reflection, having a nervous breakdown made me far more empathetic, understanding and humble. It has also helped me to help others, and I hope I have helped you in your journey to recovery.

I can't take the credit for my strength through difficult times, because God is my strength. He is who I run to in my times of trouble, who I cling to when things feel hopeless. I have learned to praise God through my storms, and the tougher the situation, the more I put my confidence and trust in Him. This again sounds so easy when you are writing it down, but less easy to put into practice! Earlier in this book I said that you might be tempted to think I am stronger than you, or someone special. My answer to you is a resounding no! It is only through Jesus that I am strong. I am ordinary, but through Him I can accomplish extraordinary things.

I pray that God will be your comfort, strength and hope during this difficult time, and that you will have courage to face the day. Take hope from my story, and believe that you will too be well, healthy and whole once again.

Acknowledgments

I want to say thank you to some special people who supported me through my journey to recovery. Firstly I want to thank my husband who, after getting over the initial shock of his wife being ill, was amazing! Thank you so much Andy for loving me and supporting me.

Secondly I want to thank my friend Rebecca Southgate Williams, who is the lovely friend I have referred to throughout this book, and who helped me so much on my journey to recovery. I also want to thank Claire Corley for her support and prayers during this very difficult time.

Thank you Jackie Olsen for giving me your professional opinion and feedback. Also a big thank you to Rebecca once again for taking the time to proof read this book and for correcting my many grammatical mistakes!

Finally thank you to all my wonderful friends and family for continuing to love and support me through my difficult times, and for being in my life. I am blessed to have so many special friends, who are too numerous to thank individually, but who are always there for me.

Useful Resources

Websites:

www.nopanic.org.uk

This is a great website with many resources; a telephone helpline, online groups you can join and a one to one mentorship scheme, plus leaflets covering many topics.

www.mind.org.uk

www.nhs.co.uk

Books:

Self Help For Your Nerves – Dr Claire Weekes

Essential Help For Your Nerves – Dr Claire Weekes

Nutrition Books:

The Optimum Nutrition Bible – Patrick Holford

Nutrition: A Practical Approach – Suzanne Le Quesne

Phone Numbers:

Samaritans – Call from any phone, at any time free of charge. The Number is 116 123

No Panic Helpline – Open from 10am to 10pm. The number is 0844 967 4848

References

Introduction

(1)   Toy Story. 2003 (Film). John Lasseter. Dir. USA. Pixar Animation Studios.

(2)   Finding Nemo. 1993 (Film). Andrew Stanton. Dir. USA. Pixar Animation Studios.

Chapter Two.

(1)   Weekes, Dr. C. (1995) Self Help for Your Nerves: Learn to relax and enjoy life again by overcoming stress and fear.UK. Harper Collins Publishers Ltd

(2)   No Panic (2018) Viewed 2004. www.nopanic.org.uk

(3)   Weekes, Dr. C. (2000) Essential Help For Your Nerves: Recover from Nervous Fatigue and Overcome Stress and Fear. UK. Thorsons, an imprint of Harper Collins Publishers Ltd

(4)   The Wizard of Oz. 1939 (Film). Victor Fleming. Dir. U.S.A. Metro-Goldwyn-Meyer.

(5)   Weekes, Dr. C. (2000) Essential Help For Your Nerves: Recover from Nervous Fatigue and Overcome Stress and Fear. UK. Thorsons, an imprint of Harper Collins Publishers Ltd

Chapter Four.

(1)   Weekes, Dr. C. (1995) Self Help for Your Nerves: Learn to relax and enjoy life again by overcoming stress and fear.UK. Harper Collins Publishers Ltd

(2)   Weekes, Dr. C. (2000) Essential Help For Your Nerves: Recover from Nervous Fatigue and Overcome Stress and Fear. UK. Thorsons, an imprint of Harper Collins Publishers Ltd

(3)   "Whether you think you can, or you think you can't--you're right." Henry Ford

Chapter Five

(1)   Weekes, Dr. C. (1995) Self Help for Your Nerves: Learn to relax and enjoy life again by overcoming stress and fear.UK. Harper Collins Publishers Ltd & Weekes, Dr. C. (2000) Essential Help For Your Nerves: Recover from Nervous Fatigue and Overcome Stress and Fear. UK. Thorsons, an imprint of Harper Collins Publishers Ltd

Chapter Six

(1)   Franklin D. Roosevelt "The only thing we have to fear is fear itself".

Chapter Eight

(1)   Finding Nemo. 1993 (Film). Andrew Stanton. Dir. USA. Pixar Animation Studios.

Chapter Twelve

(1)   Pirates of the Caribbean: The Curse Of The Black Pearl. 2003 (Film). Gore Verbinski. Dir. Walt Disney Pictures.

Chapter Fifteen

(1)   "So take a new grip with your tired hands and strengthen your weak knees". Hebrews Chapter 12 v 12, The Bible. New Living Translation

(2)   "And we know that God causes everything to work together for the good of those who love God and are called according to his purpose for them." Romans Chapter 8 v 28. The Bible. New Living Translation.

Printed in Great Britain
by Amazon